Life transformir

Nuclear powered resilience

the single golden habit that delivers amazing inner strength and comfort, enabling you to absorb and drive through life's turbulence

Combining neuroplasticity, habit forming and the universal power of Unconditional Love - to give your mind the ultimate resilience, resolve and fortitude, also bringing comfort to troubling past events without needing to examine or explore them

By Matt Sturgess

Nuclear powered resilience

ISBN: 9798371004215

CONTENTS

FOREWORD

Sometimes in life, someone comes along and does something extraordinary that changes our lives. At times that event can be spectacular – like an extravaganza and at other times, the event goes almost unnoticed – like a whisper in the breeze. Either way, the effect on us can be life-changing.

With the relatively recent advent of MRI brain scans for research purposes, we are now beginning to get a far better insight into the inner workings of the brain and the rapid developments in the whole field of neuroplasticity. We now understand that our rather 'fixed' notion of how memories and their associated emotions are stored in the brain is more or less completely 'wrong.' As a seasoned therapist, I had to admit that this all came as a kind of a shock to learn that much of what I relied on in my years of training is now more or less redundant and yet happily superseded by something far more powerful, 'agile,' and relevant. I believe our greater understanding of brain functioning, especially in the area of neuroplasticity, is nothing short of a tectonic shift in the continental plates of our understanding of human behaviour and how emotions are actually 'constructed' and is going to have an ever-increasing impact on the effectiveness of modern psychotherapies. This is, indeed, good news for anyone suffering from any kind of long-term emotional distress, mental illness,

PTSD, or simply being 'stuck' with the same debilitating emotional response to life situations. The inevitable impact on psychotherapy is akin to the advent of, say, Electric Vehicles – a massive rethink on something so familiar to us all – and yet the implications of how that technology will trickle down into our everyday lives will be no different from the growing effectiveness of the wonderful cohort of mental wellness practitioners out there in our communities.

The advent of neuroplasticity trickles down into our everyday lives. It has inevitably led to a welcome tranche of new publications, many of which report happily on the impact of their findings and are, indeed, most welcome and informative. Many practitioners and methodologies already incorporate the implications of these findings into their daily work in mental health, either implicitly (because several modern therapeutic methodologies naturally incorporate some of the new findings), or else explicitly. In the midst of this turbulent sea of therapy techniques and exciting, new research findings, it is difficult to find a simple 'user-guide' to the whole state of affairs that brings us up to date. So, it was with great relief and excitement that I discovered that my good friend Matt Sturgess had written such a guide, managing to incorporate the best of modern psychotherapeutic techniques and the latest understanding of neuroplasticity. In my opinion, Matt is unique in having so much intellect, empathy, passion, and caring poured into him. The resultant outpouring is this wonderful new book, one of many to come, I am sure. Matt has a style of writing that simply amazes me in his ability to present complex and far-reaching topics with simplicity and sparkle that catches your breath. Quite simply, Matt writes beautifully. He has also structured the book to be a straightforward read-through and, at the same time, you can return and refer, quickly finding a topic that you want to refresh in your mind. The style of this book is almost unique, and is an utterly refreshing approach to 'wellness, and enables this kind of subject matter to be accessible to everyone.

So, alongside the 'extravaganza' of the explosion of modern neuroplasticity, we have the 'whisper in the breeze' of Matt's new book. On reflection, knowing all the talent and passion poured into Matt, I shouldn't have been so surprised that his first book was this good. I really cannot wait for his next one.

Anthony Conry

B.Sc. D.H.P.

ACKNOWLEDGEMENTS

The most appropriate acknowledgement in this book is to the two people that first taught me the power of unconditional love by providing an endless supply of it – Mum and Dad. In more than one way, they were and are the architects of this book by demonstrating the power of unconditional love and nurturing me to be able to be inquisitive, combined with my passion and purpose in life to help people.

I am incredibly grateful for the endless unconditional love I receive from my girls. Without their support and love, I would have achieved far less in life and not been able to endure so much of the tough stuff in life's journey.

I must also acknowledge and thank my friend who adopted this technique, which they lovingly refer to as "The Process." I am grateful I dared to share it with them one snowy wintery day, and they were humble enough to adopt it straight away in a way that has transformed them.

1. WHY SHOULD I TAKE TIME OUT TO READ THIS?

T his is the most critical place to start; why should you bother to invest some time in yourself to read this?

How often in an average day do you feel an inner glow? An absolute, profound feeling of love and warmth, regardless of what is happening to you. A feeling in which you are firmly anchored to an unbreakable truth that you are loved, and whatever life throws at you, it will be ok because you have something no one can ever take away from you, unbounded, Unconditional Love.

After reading this book, you will learn many things, and the three most important lessons will be,

1. **Nuclear-powered resilience** - a simple, comprehensive technique that will give you the inner resilience of a nuclear-powered machine that will bring balance and comfort to any situation, real (from the past or present) or imagined future fear.

2. **How to make resilience a habit** - a simple way of continuously and effortlessly increasing the ability to become resilient towards life's events, by enabling the

ability to glide through life with less mental ballast, that was previously holding you back.

3. **Invaluable knowledge**: An understanding of the mind's workings and the opportunities it provides when you harness it.

I am a highly rational and sceptical person who started his career as an analytical, pragmatic engineer. That part of my character has not changed, nor has my curiosity about how things work. I share the technique based on science, practical experience, and personal insight. Its simplicity makes it even more powerful, when you embrace this philosophy it will change your life. If you allow your scepticism or fear of the unknown to get in your way, that is your choice. But do yourself a favour and stop limiting yourself, get out of your own way! Give this a try, it could just be the best thing you ever did.

All my life, I have been driven by a single purpose to help others, which I have done from time to time but not on a scale that meets my personal desire to help thousands of people enjoy a better life. After years of building my curiosity about how the mind works, how we create habits, the power of neuroplasticity, and one significant piece of personal learning, I realised that I had a simple technique that could help anyone. One day I was brave enough to share my technique with a friend in need of help; they were suffering from mental trauma, depression, and an ongoing lifetime of underlying discomfort. In unison, all of these reasons

6

became an undercurrent that affected them throughout their lives, and in response, I shared with them the technique that I wrote in this book, it changed them forever. The change in them was remarkable within twenty-four hours after adopting the method, it may not be that quick with everyone, but the opportunity is there. Will you take it?

This technique is simple to use. Do not be fooled into thinking it is not powerful because of its simplicity. It appears simple because it taps into how our minds work, I have spent many years reading and studying how the mind works, so you do not have to. This and my insight into what granted me mental stability has helped me connect to the science of neuroplasticity, habit-forming, and a knowledge of how our minds operate.

My sceptical brain always asks after I have read a book, or heard a speaker talk, *'So what?'* Often, I might think that was fascinating or even brilliant. But my *'So what?'* question brings me back to reality, asking my brain effectively

"So, what is in it for me?",

"What will be different and what and how can I implement this?"

If I cannot answer these questions, the information I received was just interesting rather than actionable. So, what will you get from this?

1.1 KNOWLEDGE

An understanding of how our minds work. If you are curious like me and need to understand how something works to be able to adopt it, then this is for you. If you are the type of person that thinks that's all boring, I respect that you can then skip this part of the book, which I have made easy to do.

1.2 TWO TYPES OF RESILIENCE

1. **Building resilience** - If you follow the habit-forming part of the technique, you will continually increase your mental resilience, so when a storm comes, you will be like a ship that effortlessly sails through the big waves with the inner knowledge that you gained, thus embracing the strength that it gives you.

2. **Instant turbo boost resilience** - A technique that allows you to boost your resilience on demand, to feel good and release endorphins or help cope with life's sporadic, more intensive events and challenges.

1.3 HEALING FOR PAST TRAUMAS

The ability to neutralise the debilitating effect of past traumas or events, as I helped my friend do.

The brilliant part of this technique is that you never need to go anywhere near your past traumas in your mind. There is absolutely no need to try and understand, explain, or examine such events. The beauty of this technique is that it acts like a universal healer for all and any past, current, or future situations or events that might cause mental discomfort.

So, what are you waiting for? Let's get ready to learn and apply it on our daily lives.

2. How to Use Your Book

Getting the most out of your book and the technique written within is essential. To ensure you get the transformation you yearn for, understanding the book's layout and designs will make it easier to navigate.

I will also talk you through how to maximise the benefit, depending on if you are reading the book for the first time or dipping back into the book to cover a specific topic.

We all have different styles of learning, like me, many appreciate details and explanations of a subject matter while others will prefer a more concise, *'get on with it'* approach. I have set the book out in a way that can accommodate both learning styles.

2.1 Layout

To enable navigation through the book more manageable, we will run through the layout I have used.

Key Concepts

When I introduce certain concepts, I will highlight their core concept, which makes things easier when rereading the book.

A dotted border will surround the Key Concepts, here is a visual example.

```
Key concept

90-95% of our activities, responses, and thoughts are
unconscious, preprogramed habits or autopilots.
```

As you would expect, this sets out a key idea, so they stand out and provides a to-the-point summary when reading the book on subsequent visits.

If you are in a hurry or do not want to read, key facts are the best way of getting the critical nuggets from the book.

So what?

Whenever I have listened to someone speak or have read something, one of the self-talk mantras in my head is *'So what?'* For me, the critical test lies when I have received some summarised information.

"How can I use this?"

The phrase *'So what?'* is a shortcut that allows me to think.

"How can I make this relevant to me? What do I actually need to do to make this happen."

In the 'So what?' section, I record the actions you need to take to create changes in your life. The 'So what?' section can be identified by the greyed-out text and the heading of the section is highlighted.

Here is an example,

So what?

Remember to focus on schedules, not deadlines or outcomes. You do not have complete control over an outcome, you do have control over how often and for how long you schedule an activity. For example, you decide you want to run a five-kilometre race in less than thirty minutes and have not run for many years. You can set yourself a schedule to walk or run thrice a week for five minutes, which can be adjusted as time passes. This schedule outcome will help you develop a running habit until it has increased to five kilometres in thirty minutes.

Theory

I strongly need to understand how things work, not everyone shares that trait. I do not use a lot of theory in the book from time to time and I like to include some supporting explanations based on science and research.

These theory sections will be denoted with a bold heading and the text will be written in italics inside a bounded area to easily distinguish them from the rest of the text, for example as shown below in a visual form.

Theory

At the base of the brain, we all have an area called the Reticular Activating System (RAS) which filters out all the new information received, thus allowing you to focus on what you tell your mind fixates on. by where you place your attention with thoughts. If you consider, we have millions of pieces of information coming at our brains from our senses. If we were consciously aware of this process, we would drown in the information and thus be paralysed by it. Imagine if a superhero had the power of keen hearing! If they did not learn how to focus on one voice at a time, they would go crazy from hearing so many things all at once.

Summary

At the end of each chapter, you will find a helpful summarised revision of the chapter and its contents.

2.2 LEARNING STYLES

We are all wired slightly differently, which is equally valid regarding learning styles of consuming information. One of the most significant differences in learning style is if you like detail or not. My personality trait enjoys detail and understanding how things work and why. I fully recognise that people with different personality traits get bored quickly with detail and want to get to the point quickly.

Whether you are reading the book for the first time or dipping into it again, I have designed the book so you could skip the more theoretical parts or find the critical parts by just focussing on the 'Key concepts,' The actionable *'So what?'* parts and the summary section will be located at the end of each chapter.

2.3 RE-READING THE BOOK

If you have already read the book once, going through it a second time should be easy by recapping and simply focussing your attention on the following sections and the summary at the end of the chapters.

- Theory
- So What?

- Key Concept

3. WHAT IS THE BASIS OF THIS TECHNIQUE?

T he good thing for you is that I have done a lot of reading on a series of related topics for many years, to piece this technique together, so you do not have to. In essence, it is a combination of **neuroplasticity** which is the science behind how we can change ourselves

+ Understanding how the **unconscious** mind works.

+ Understanding the **language** of the Unconscious mind.

+ Learning from experts how to create **habits.**

+ Harnessing and embracing the power of **Unconditional Love.**

3.1 SYNOPSIS

Here is a quick rundown of the five elements above, if you want a more detailed explanation, read on in the next chapter. You can skip that chapter if you want to get straight into the technique and how it works

3.1.1 Neuroplasticity

There has been a lot of study into the Neuroplasticity of the mind with modern brain scans to prove what, many cultures, have believed for centuries based on observation.

In the context of this book, the key takeaways from Neuroplasticity are the following:

- Our brains are not hard wired, we can easily create new neural pathways.

- The more we practice a set of thoughts, the more ingrained the new pathway gets in our minds.

- New neural pathways represent new responses and habits according to the situations or events in our life.

- We can create a new response to an old situation we choose to have. It requires a little knowledge, which I will share with you, along with a bit of imagination and creativity.

3.1.2 Key characteristics of the unconscious mind

In the more detailed section, I will share more about this. But the key points are these,

- There are different regions of the brain that form at different stages in a human's evolution.

- One of the more ancient parts of our brain is the unconscious part.

- The unconscious part of the brain stores all of our ingrained habits. Effectively, we create responses according to situations or events in our life. For example, how to hold a knife, hold a fork, breath, drive or ride a bike, etc.

- Once you get a habit lodged in the unconscious, it will occur when triggered to do so. It will not question the logic of executing the habit, whereas the conscious region of your mind is the brain's rational, reasoning part. The conscious region of the mind is the gatekeeper of one's sense of initiating an action. If you speak the language of your unconscious mind, you can lodge new habits and the way to go about it is easy, you will learn it later.

- It might seem strange, but the unconscious mind responds similarly to actual and imagined events. Think about why you get emotional when watching a film, react badly to nightmares, or get anxious before an interview. Your conscious mind knows there is nothing to worry about while your unconscious does not. We will exploit this key characteristic to create Unconditional Love in your mind, regardless of the facts. **This is the most important fact for you to understand regarding the inner workings of this technique.**

Theory

How the unconscious part of the mind works:

- *Habits are executed when triggered automatically.*
- *Stores all our habitual responses according to a situation, events, and learnt responses.*
- *Responds to actual events, imagination and thoughts the same way.*

Key concept

Your unconscious mind reacts the same way to actual or imagined events, this is at the core of how this technique works.

3.1.3   Language of the unconscious mind

The unconscious mind communicates and interprets its world predominantly in pictures, mini-movies or through visual representations in our minds in combination with emotion. When you get a gut instinct, that is the unconscious mind communicating with you. When I say *'mini movie,'* I am referring to the mental theatre in our minds, where we visualise situations and run through them as if they were a movie in our minds.

I will show you how to build a simple way of communicating 'Unconditional Love' to the unconscious mind.

Key concept

Your unconscious region of the mind prefers to communicate visually with emotions attached or associated with those mental images.

3.1.4   Habit creation

Habits, as we know, are created through repetition. Once a habit is *'lodged'* in the unconscious mind, it gets activated automatically based on a specific trigger that is associated with that particular habit. The trigger is simply a situation, event, environment, or set of circumstances that the unconscious mind has learnt as the cue to initiate the habit routine.

Examples of some triggers are the following:

- When you enter your bathroom, it is dark, so you automatically reach out for the light. This response sits within the realm of unconscious mind where the trigger was the lack of light along with the location.

- You get nervous and anxious when you think about travelling near a location with bad memories, such as a hospital or a school where you got bullied. The trigger in this example is clearly the location.

- In the morning when you get dressed, what piece of clothing do you put on first? I bet this has got you puzzled, the strange thing is because habits live and operate in the unconscious part of the brain, you do them without thinking; if you wear tights, socks, or trousers, which leg do you put in first? If you have paraplegia, pay close to your routine; does it have more than one way of being achieved? Now think about what that routine is, it's challenging to recall isn't it? Think also, what is your trigger for that routine, what specifically marks the start of the routine? Sitting on your bed? Coming out of the bathroom?

Once the habit is triggered, we run through the routine without conscious thought, e.g., brushing our teeth, riding a bicycle, buttering a piece of toast etc.

Those who have researched habit creation, such as Jeremy Dean or Charles Duhigg, suggest that when creating new habits, the result of which is usually connected with a reward. One expert in this area, B.J.Fogg Ph.D. and the author of Tiny Habits, suggests an anchor different from a reward. An anchor is to be performed instantaneously after the habit routine is completed. Usually, it is simply a mental platitude in your head like "well done," "that was great," "another perfect execution of my habit," and in combination with a physical gesture like a fist pump or a little jump in the air.

Key concept

Habit creation consists of

- A trigger for the habit to kick in.
- The habit routine itself.
- A simple word and or physical reward anchor.
- Repetition to embed a new habit.

3.1.5   Unconditional Love

You could break this technique down into two things; the first is knowing how the mind works so you can implant the benefits of Unconditional Love, regardless of your reality. The second part is appreciating and understanding what Unconditional Love is and why it is so powerful.

Let's address the question: *what is Unconditional Love?* For me, it is obvious because I am fortunate enough to have experienced this. Sadly, for others, this is something they have had little or no experience of.

What is Unconditional Love, in my opinion?

> "Knowing that someone or more than one person
> absolutely loves you comes what may."

Knowing that you are wanted and loved regardless of what you do or say is very powerful. That constant undeniable truth of absolute acceptance and love is like having a nuclear-powered, deeply embedded inner knowing. I shared that emotion with my parents, who demonstrated their love daily by being there for my brother and me in their actions, words, and deeds—things like always coming to school events and parents' evenings without fail. My dad made time to make toys for me with his hands and heart receiving numerous hugs from my mum. Knowing my parents would take on anyone or anything to protect my brother and me, positively impacted our confidence. Don't get me wrong, we had disagreements and tantrums as kids, but it always came back to that common denominator of Unconditional Love.

Love without conditions, selfless, open, and most important, no obligations attached to it is what stands for Unconditional Love.

It is a cliché, but the message is true and powerful, we all want to be wanted and loved. That inner, unflinching truth of knowing you are unconditional loved will help you power through life's challenges because when the chips are down, you know you are loved, without question. Even those who say they don't need love are convincing themselves otherwise. Unconditional Love gives you a mental bedrock to bounce back from and limits you from experiencing the extreme lows of one's life. Regularly practising this technique will provide a cushion for your subconscious, ensuring that the low points are mitigated when tough times arrive, so you are not knocked to your knees.

The beauty of this technique is that you can create Unconditional Love in your mind, as the unconscious part of the mind accepts what you present to it. It behaves the same way with real or imagined scenarios. This is regardless of the facts of your life up until now and if, you are like me, and have had the immense benefit of Unconditional Love, then you can learn how to fully tap into that emotion and enhance your life's quality. To be clear, this technique is not limited to those who have little exposure to Unconditional Love — those who have experienced Unconditional Love in the past can also benefit from this technique.

I must also make it clear to my amazing family, comprised of my wife, daughter and cats, that my origins of Unconditional Love came from my childhood but have been enhanced immeasurably by their Unconditional Love of me. For that, I am truly and eternally grateful. But the excellent learning point is those of us who are fortunate to have this need to know how to tap into it and enhance it. It is way too easy in our busy lives not entirely to capitalise on what we may already have.

Those with little or no Unconditional Love can finally have this in a specific and unique way.

4. INSIGHTS INTO HOW OUR MINDS WORK

T hose who wish to understand and enjoy the process of digging into how and why things happen will find this chapter incredibly insightful. As a person, I need to understand concepts before I accept and use this. If you want to jump to the core technique, you could skip this chapter and move on, the choice is yours.

Our minds are incredibly powerful, we are on the cusp of understanding their inner workings and increasingly using science to prove many ancient concepts along with techniques that have been used for centuries to manage our minds.

The simple truth, as a species, is that we get lots of things done therein, our minds have developed numerous routines to simplify and automate our lives to assist us in getting these things done.

Television quiz shows often say that the answer is easy if you know it! A silly but true saying. When we understand how something works and how to change it, the mystery of the

26

unknown is removed thus, tasks suddenly become possible. What seemed difficult or impossible becomes a simple routine.

A routine takes a huge amount of mental processing power every day. A simple task like pouring a glass of water then, drinking it requires calculations and processing of sensory data. Alongside drinking a glass of water, we must control our heart, breathing and countless other bodily functions that keep us alive. Then we get into our daily activities like getting showered, dressed, daily commute, and our work. Just stop for a minute and make a mental note of all the activities you complete daily. Now take one of those activities and consider how long it took you to learn and assess what goes into making that activity take place. Add to that an awareness that you are receiving a constant stream of information from your five senses while all this is going on. For those that have lost the ability of one or more senses, the remaining senses become keener, thus bombarding them with a myriad of information.

Just considering,

- Daily survival body functions like breathing.
- Daily routines.
- The flood of continuous information from our senses.

You start to build an awareness and appreciation of how much is going on in our lives. You can add other layers to this analogy to build a complete picture of what our minds process daily. Yet overall, we get on with stuff and many days feel the same as the previous days. This is because our minds have developed a range of processes to simplify and automate our lives. Without such mechanisms, our minds would be overwhelmed and have no guidance on what to focus on. Therefore, managing daily activities will become difficult.

With science and research, we are becoming more aware of how our minds manage our lives and simplify things for us, streamlining our awareness from an almost infinite realm of information to a narrow, relevant set.

By explaining some of these mechanisms, we can use this knowledge to help automate our lives, with our conscious choices of how we would choose to go forward rather than just happening of its own accord.

I will briefly cover the following points from the section mentioned above:

- The characteristics of the conscious and unconscious parts of the mind.
- How we form and go about our habits.
- Neuroplasticity is defined as the growing science of neural connections in the brain and how we form new skills.

Theory

Conscious and unconscious parts of the mind

During the evolution of the human brain, our brains have developed considerably, although there is still a lot to understand. Numerous models explain the different functions of our brains and the responsibility of each area.

It is not the scope of this book to cover the vast amount of research in this area, I will summarise the key relevant points. Increasingly, we appreciate that we have three significant points of evolution of our brains. The earliest parts of our brains control essential functions such as breathing, swallowing, heart rate, blood pressure, consciousness, and emotion. This part of the brain is known as the archipallium or the brain stem, which sits at the base of the brain connected to the spinal cord, often referred to as the reptilian brain.

The next significant evolution is connected to developing the emotional interpretation of our drive, motivation, and the need for social bonding or belonging. Responsible for these functions is the limbic system or paleopallium.

Recently, in terms of millions of years of brain evolution, the neocortex or neo-mammalian brain region manages reasoning, understanding time, empathy, language, and socially conscious. You can read more about this in Ruby Wax's book "Frazzled".

When considering emotions and how we process them, Ruby Wax's book describes how they start in the brain stem, the limbic region, then continue to acknowledge, process, and register the emotion for future reference. Then the neocortex decides what to do when the emotion has been evaluated.

I want to draw your awareness to the so-called unconscious and conscious parts of the brain. We do not know for certain, but the characteristics of the unconscious parts of the brain are associated with the earliest parts of the brain's evolution, with the conscious part of the brain being associated with the more recent neocortex.

I will share with you the characteristics of the conscious and unconscious parts of the brain, these characteristics will have relevance as to why the techniques I share with you in the book work.

Just a quick side point, some people refer to the unconscious part of the mind as the subconscious, it is the same part of the mind with a different name. I prefer the term unconscious since it better describes a powerful part of the mind just whirring away in the background. The subconscious somehow creates an image of a lesser amount of the mind when the unconscious could be argued to be the more powerful part.

Characteristics

Conscious

- *Uses reasoning to evaluate.*
- *Processes in words, language, and images.*
- *Processes forty bits of info per second.*
- *Can retain 7+/-2 tasks, multiplexing between each one as it can only process or focus on one task at a time.*
- *Active when awake, dormant when asleep.*
- *Operates short-term and frequently used memories*
- *Act as a logical gatekeeper to stop "unsuitable" requests or information from entering the unconscious.*
- *They are not fully developed until we are about seven years old.*

Unconscious

- *Logical and absolute (no reasoning, accepts what information it has a being real.)*
- *Cannot distinguish between imaginary and real images, thoughts, or emotions*
- *Processes in images and emotion*
- *Communicates in emotion*
- *Processes four million bits of information per second*
- *Always active and from the start of our lives*
- *Controls habits and vital routines such as breathing*
- *Stores all your memories as images, emotions, and symbols*
- *Cannot process negative images and words*

> • *Directly accessible when the conscious reasoning mind rests,*
> *during, just before, and after sleep, when daydreaming or tired*

The key takeaways are that most of our brain's activities occur in the unconscious, with habits that are engrained and become unconscious reactions to situations. Many of these habits are adopted at a young age, between two to six years and often are not relevant to our lives as adults. What you observed and were exposed to up to the age of about seven forms your *'rule book'* of principles and values. This technique can reset that compass if you choose to.

> **Key concept**
>
> The conscious and unconscious parts of the mind operate very differently. The powerhouse is the unconscious mind. When we harness this, with the habits or autopilots that fit our current needs and conscious choices, we can automate control of how we respond to events, rather accept learnt behaviour that may not fit our current requirements, or the information gained in our youth.

In the theory explained above, I have given you a glimpse into how our minds are constructed. We like to group things to provide explanations by using models of the real world. Models are approximations and simplifications of what we think is going on in our environment. The brain and mind are hugely powerful and complex instruments. Our understanding of the physical characteristics and the hidden psychological aspects of the mind is growing, quite often confirming what scholars and various cultures have worked out from trial and error over thousands of years. There is no clear cut-off between the unconscious and conscious minds or clear physical boundaries of the three generations of our brains, it is more nuanced than that. But the learning we have from these models helps us understand more, it is this knowledge that is invaluable in being able to speak the "language" of our brains or minds, to be able to effectively reprogram ourselves to enjoy our lives more and help us achieve our aims in life.

I could share a lot of information about the characteristics of the unconscious and conscious parts of the mind, but I want to draw the reader's attention to the ability of the unconscious mind to automate much of what we do with habits or mini autopilots, that helps us perform so many activities almost without thinking. That's another reason we call this part of the mind the unconscious. Research has shown that when habits are ingrained, they engage little with emotion and we enact the habits almost invisibly, with little to no awareness or acknowledgement. Charles Duhigg explains this in his book, 'The Power of Habit.'

The other key point is that our unconscious mind responds similarly to actual and imagined events. This is the key as to why this technique works.

The science of neuroplasticity has been developing fast. In essence, this shows how we learn, store memories, and create new habits. We do this by creating new neural pathways with collections of neurons. Phrases like *"I am stuck in a rut"* are more valid than we realised. As neural pathways are well-trodden mental pathways that we could imagine as ruts. Neuroplasticity shows how we can learn new habits and embed them in our lives.

Emotions are used to keep us safe from real or perceived threats. Our unconscious mind does not have the ability to reason and consider, as does our conscious mind. As a result, our unconscious mind responds to actual events the same way as it does to imagined events. For example, if you relive a past event, the emotion will automatically come to you. Even if you know that it is not real, it is a memory, but emotion impacts you all the same. When you watch a film, you may get tense, cry, or worried, you know it is not real, but you react as if it was. When you dream, your conscious mind is suspended, but your unconscious mind is alert. You respond to dreams emotionally as if they were real.

Referring to how emotions can distort our sense of reality and truth, our emotions are responses to existing or perceived threats. Because our emotions are genuine, we can get tricked into thinking an emotional response is based on truth and reality when it could equally be a response to an imagined event. For example, let's think about a presentation that we must give, if our programming is that giving presentations is difficult or unpleasant, when we think about doing this, unpleasant emotions kick in. These emotions are designed to protect us from what we fear, so we do not risk being in danger. In our rational conscious mind, we know no real harm can come from giving a presentation, but our unconscious mind does not know the difference between real and imagined events.

To develop this critical point by acknowledging that we respond to the movies, we create in our minds the same way we react to the real world. In fact, it is the unconscious part of our mind that does this, the rational conscious part of the mind knows the difference between reality and imagination, but the unconscious part does not. Our conscious mind is not active when we sleep and decreases in activity as we awaken, as we go towards sleep and when we daydream... Scientists have also found a collection of neurons in the brain that they refer to as mirror neurons. These neurons appear to be part of our learning and empathy systems, when we experience something, like watching a film, we act out the scenario in our minds and our bodies respond as if it were real. For example, we see someone running, our heart rate might increase a little. This is a way of trying out, practicing, or learning a new experience.

Imagine holding a big juicy lemon in your hands, make the image clear, see the classic shape of a lemon and the vibrant yellow of its skin. Notice the texture of its surface when you touch the skin of the lemon in your mind. Now imagine getting a sharp knife and cutting through the succulent lemon, all the juices run out as you do so. Pick up one half of the lemon and bring it to your mouth, bite into the juicy lemon. What do you notice? You probably noticed the sourness of the lemon in your mouth. But this is just your imagination!

The language of the unconscious mind is predominantly pictures or images and emotions. It is the conscious mind that works more with words.

So what?

Here are some useful guidance notes on how the unconscious processes information and is therefore how it communicates. Think of it like a computer, you use the keyboard or voice control to communicate with the Central Processing Unit (CPU) the heart of the computer. The keyboard equivalent for the unconscious mind, is creating images and pictures in your mind sending and sensing emotions.

1. **Images** – using pictures or images in your mind is a great way of telling your unconscious mind what you are interested in. Movement is even better for those mental images, so a mini movie running through your mind is a great way to communicate what you want, to your unconscious mind.

2. **Do not use negatives!** – your unconscious mind cannot process negatives, so focus your thoughts on what you want, not what you do not want. For example, if you are worried about getting ill, do not focus your thoughts along the lines of *'I hope I do not get ill,'* because this just creates an image an instruction that you want to be ill. Instead focus your thoughts on an image of good health or <u>what you do want.</u> If you are questioning my statement about not being able to process negatives, try not thinking about a pink Elephant! You need to create the image of what you do not want to think about, don't you?

3. **Emotion** – if you can use positive emotions of happiness or love, you can better use the mind's ability of focusing. Your unconscious communicates to you through emotions like the gut feeling you sometimes get. Feelings and emotions are extremely powerful.

4. **Memory techniques** – if you have read about how to memorise things, you will be aware its more effective to make mental images colourful, dynamic, ideally moving and abstract objects. Ideally, these images can be a bit exaggerated and

action orientated, this is because you are using the communication language of the unconscious mind.

If you are reading this and are concerned about the quality of mental images and mini-movies, do not concern yourself. Mine are not that vivid, others are much better at this than me but practise will improve this. For many, me included, the mini movies are not like watching a film but more a combination of sensations, feelings and fleeting images.

The single most important discovery about neuroplasticity is that we can change the 'wiring' in our brains. This means we can change our habits, our responses to situations and the emotions we attach to memories. This is fundamental to what I will share with you in this book.

To speed up decision making and leave our conscious minds to consider new or more challenging issues, our unconscious has registered millions of habits. I choose to use the term 'embed,' to describe how our unconscious minds take on new habits. These habits are mini subroutines that are triggered under certain circumstances through our unconscious mind. You have probably been aware of this perhaps when driving somewhere and for a moment you were lost in a daydream until, you suddenly become conscious of where you are thus, realising that you had no conscious memory of the last five minutes or so. That is because your unconscious mind was on autopilot, driving the car for you.

If you acknowledge the constant activity of your brain, then it is a wonder that we ever get anything done! Of the total time our minds spend processing stimuli then, five to ten percent of it is done with the conscious mind with ninety to ninety-five percent taking place in the unconscious mind. Research has shown that the conscious part of our mind has limited capacity and works far slower than the unconscious mind, we can only process one task or thought at a time in our conscious realm. When people talk about multitasking, on the broader sense the word does not make sense and is false since, we multiplex. Multiplexing is the act of rapidly switching from one thought or task to another; it happens so quickly that it feels like we are doing multiple tasks at the same time. As I shared earlier, research shows our conscious minds can only hold between five and nine tasks or thoughts at a time, whereas our unconscious minds seem to have infinite capacity to run many mini subroutines simultaneously.

You could argue we can multitask, but only with the unconscious part of the mind.

How does our unconscious mind pick up so many habits? Each time we learn a task like reading a book, driving a car, or typing on a computer, it gets stored as learning in our unconscious minds. Because the unconscious mind has so much more capacity for processing and is much faster than our conscious mind, we constantly call on the little learnt programs or habits of our unconscious minds to make everyday activities happen automatically. This way the limited capacity our conscious minds have, can be used for learning new tasks or those requiring concentration, problem-solving or logic.

Our unconscious mind looks for cues to trigger these habits. These cues are circumstances or a specific environment that triggers the habit pattern. For example, if you enter your bathroom, you automatically reach for the light chord when it's dark. The cue was simply the location and the fact that it was dark. When you get out of bed, this situation triggers your habits as to what you do next, according to your regular routine. If you have to think which foot you put into your socks, trousers, skirt or tights first, you probably cannot remember. But in fact, you always lead with the same foot. This equally applies to someone with an artificial limb, they will continue to lead with their lead foot each time because this habit is stored deep in the unconscious; hence you will find it challenging to recall which foot you lead with. Next time you get dressed, pause and consider which foot leads first and then stop to lead with the other foot. Sense how your conscious mind now has to be engaged – it feels downright 'strange' and different.

Here is another example of learnt behaviour buried in the unconscious mind that you are unaware of. Consider when you cross your arms, which hand is closer to your chest, without crossing your arms. Now, if it is safe to do so, cross your arms. Close your eyes and observe which hand is closer to your chest and which one is outside when you fold your arms? I bet you have no idea until you practically experimented. Now try and fold your arms the other way round, lead with the other arm. It feels weird and more complex, yes?

As part of our capability to get things done, we have countless beliefs stored in the unconscious minds that run little subroutines for us. A belief is simply a set of learnt "rules" that we use to simplify our lives. If we recognise a situation we have met before or similar to past learning, our habits, or self-beliefs kick, to make life easier for us by making and executing automated decisions. Many of our beliefs can be especially useful, some however hold us back. Because our beliefs are so embedded in our unconscious, we often do not notice they are there and they act as a set of silent rules by which we run our lives. Self-limiting beliefs are purely the programming we have given ourselves from past experiences that inhibits us from doing some things in our lives.

Theory

How we form and use habits

An astonishing amount of ongoing research has gone into how we create habits, how long it takes and what is happening physically in the brain when we develop habits. There is a lot you can read on this, here is a practical summary.

As adults, there are two major mechanisms for forming habits,

1. **Trauma** – if a major event takes place in your life that has a powerful enough emotional effect, it can create an almost instantaneous habit. Habit is maybe a misleading label as it's more of a programmed response to help you avoid a situation like the one that was traumatic.

2. **Repetition** -we all know from our school days that a good way to remember a lesson is to learn by rote.

Most of our habits get embedded by repetition. What we do in the physical world when creating habits translates into new neural pathways in our brains. The often-used phrase, "I am stuck in a rut," has a lot of scientific merits as you could conceive a neural pathway that defines a given habit as being like a well-trodden path or rut.

How long does it take to create a habit?

Many books indicate it depends on the habit, but it usually takes about twenty-one days. In Jeremy Dean's book "Making habits breaking habits," he refers to research carried out at University College London with 96 participants that took between 20 and 84 days for habits to become automatic. On average, it took 66 days for habits to become fully embedded.

In fact, it has been shown that we can embed habits quickly if we choose an existing cue or trigger or choose a simple task therein, adding complexity once the routine is established. For example, I decided to start doing push-ups, I used the trigger of brushing my teeth in the morning to start it. The minute I put the toothbrush down, I started doing push-ups. I set an easy target of two push-ups. Within a few days, I kept doing more because I wanted to, and it was easy. Within a week and a half, I was up to fifteen; I could do twenty by two weeks. By week three, I was up to thirty!

We will cover habit formation in more detail later, but for now, here is a glimpse of how to create new habits or modify existing habits according to Charles Duhigg, in his book "The power of habit -Why we do what we do and how to change."

Charles talks about three key stages to habit creation:

*1 **Cue** – a trigger as to when the habit will start. This could be a specific time, an event, e.g., an email arriving to a location, or a situation*

*2. **Routine** – the actual habit itself, the things we think or do that define the habit*

*3. **Reward** – some form of reward for completing the routine, which could be a chemical endorphin rush after exercising, praising yourself, or rewarding yourself like taking a break*

In BJ Fogg's Ph.D. book, "Tiny Habits", he clearly distinguishes the reward. His research has shown that reward, or "celebration," as he calls it, should happen immediately after the habit has been performed. The celebration "wires" the habit by feeling good. The celebration can be as simple as telling yourself "well done", "good job" or something similar and accompanied by a simply celebratory physical gesture link a fist pump.

Understanding how habits are formed and can be changed will be useful so that we can program into the unconscious part of our mind with our new chosen automatic response. A response we designed with conscious, rational, reasoning thought.

Summary

Our conscious minds are the part that is rational, problem-solving and can consider context but has a limited capacity to focus on multiple subjects.

Our unconscious minds operate much faster than our conscious minds and have a vast store of learning and habits to simplify and manage our lives. Our unconscious minds do not have a reason; they operate without question and process thoughts as images and emotions.

Our brains have evolved with three distinct regions of evolution, the area of the brain most associated with the unconscious is associated with the earlier parts of brain evolution, which grew before we started speaking as a species. Hence the unconscious mind's mode of communication is predominantly images and emotions.

The unconscious mind accepts the information as if it was real and reacts similarly to imaginary thoughts. We know this instinctively when we respond emotionally to a film or a dream, our conscious, rational mind knows it is not true, but we still react to it like it is true.

We also discovered the key elements of how habits are formed, starting with a trigger or cue to start it, which is then embedded into our routine. When developing a habit, we should give ourselves a positive stimulus with encouraging words and a physical gesture like a fist clench, this helps reinforce the habit quickly, as does repetition as well.

5. How to embed Unconditional Love

5.1   Background

I was fortunate enough to have loving parents who provided my brother and I with Unconditional Love. It was not till I was much older that I realised how much mental resilience and inner strength that action had given me. As I met others who either did not have this or had a completely opposite experience through difficult upbringings, I appreciated the benefit I had received even more. Even more importantly, I realised how that had forever impacted my life.

As I learnt more about the science of the brain and how it works, I understood that Unconditional Love is available to everyone. Independent of the facts of their lives, past or present; With the knowledge that our unconscious minds respond the same way to real or imagined thoughts, it became clear that we can design our unique Unconditional Love experience.

I have also realised that when I could help others, regardless of the specifics of what was troubling them, Unconditional Love was a form of universal fix. The beauty of applying Unconditional Love is emotion that there is no need to understand or analyse in any way the original issue, feeling or trauma that is being healed.

Unconditional Love supports us through issues or troubles that play out in our minds or through our lives.

5.2 UNCONDITIONAL LOVE

I want to teach you something extraordinary. I was inspired to include this section after helping someone overcome past trauma. From time to time, it would come back and cause them a lot of mental discomfort, affecting their performance in life. As it does with all of us, if we have something troubling us, it distracts us and can show up physically in our bodies, affecting what we do or stop doing and how we interact with others.

We all have parts of our past lives that have an impact on us. Sometimes this impact can be incredibly positive or inspiring and can also be limiting or highly debilitating. This limiting impact can constantly drag on our performance or happiness or create occasional flare-ups. In some cases, it can be entirely mentally debilitating. We also have current situations in life or future events that impact us in the same way as past events, we can also suffer from an absence of something that we feel missed out on or should have achieved.

Since our reality is what occupies the most significant chunk of our conscious minds. Our thinking affects our physiology and vice versa; the thoughts in our minds have a substantial impact on our lives. I am not undervaluing our reality's impact on our lives, but as humans, we tend to amplify and exaggerate impact with the "stories" and narratives that we create, thus stifling our observation or enjoyment of actual events. This technique is even more powerful because so much of the drama in our lives comes from what goes on in our heads. Mark Twain summed this up best with his quote,

"I have suffered a great many catastrophes in my life.
Most of them never happened"

Mark Twain's incredible quote sums up the feeling of torment regarding future scenarios that may not have occurred yet. Somehow, we invest a lot of time in conceptualising hypothetical scenarios rather than focussing on the present.

So, for whom can this technique be useful for? To be frank everyone!

Consider these scenarios,

1. **Those that have experienced Unconditional Love –**
   People like me have benefited from Unconditional Love. My most significant experience of this was when I was a child but it continues from the love of my family, my wife,

daughter and our cat. But we can benefit from a super boost like this. Additionally, Unconditional Love builds your resilience to life's events and boosts our mental capabilities for troubling times and is available to us on demand.

2. **Past trauma or no Unconditional Love, especially as a child** – having never had unconditional love can either spur people and drive them to overcome adversity or contribute to a constant feeling of self-doubt. When life throws events at you, those big challenging events in life, redundancy, divorce etc, when you need to draw on an inner strength and determination, Unconditional Love is a huge reassuring bedrock to build back from. So do not deny yourself.

3. **Everyday challenges** – every day we have challenges, some are big ones, some are just an accumulation of smaller challenges. How we respond and scale these challenges in our minds, has a big impact on our mental wellbeing. Having enhanced resilience, from Unconditional Love, helps us ride over these rough seas far more easily. Think of it like having a bigger mental "cushion" that can absorb life's challenges. Or like a really

good car suspension glides over the rut's potholes of life's journey.

5.3 FEELINGS NOT THOUGHTS

If you are affected or suffer from a particular trauma or past event in your life, some experts might suggest examining that past event. This should only be undertaken by an expert. In my experience if you start analysing such things, you are thinking about them. The mind works by clustering thoughts with similar associations, to my way of thinking this is just making the issue bigger in our minds. My experience and learning are, it is better to focus on the emotions or feeling such an event causes and imagine giving those emotions Unconditional Love. Not questioning what happened or why, simply accepting it is what it is and providing unconditional and unquestioning love in your mind, targeted on those uncomfortable **feelings** and **emotions**, not the thoughts. This is a very clear distinction. Giving love to the feelings and emotions associated with an event, not the thoughts surrounding the event.

While **watching** a Marvel heroes' episode there was a character discussing his fear before going into battle, a wise old Samurai said something along the lines of,

"When you accept death, it no longer has any power over you"

Now this is a fictional series and death is a big subject, but the point is simple. If you accept something it no longer has any power to grow into a bigger story in your head. The weird thing is often our imagination and thoughts are far more terrifying and frightening than reality for most people, yet we get trapped in this cinematic world in our heads so easily.

If negative thoughts or fears enter your mind and you struggle to move on to positive thoughts, try a different approach to "dissolve" unhelpful thoughts.

Whether you have children or not you can probably associate with the fact that hearing a baby scream continuously is very upsetting and stressful. We all know in that situation the solution is not to ignore the baby screaming, turn the music up loader, put on some headphones and hope it stops. For most people the instinct is to go to the baby see what is wrong, pick it up, cradle it and give it Unconditional Love and comfort. Yet with our own fears, we tend to hide away from them, rather than comfort ourselves, we challenge ourselves as to why we feel so bad, making ourselves feel guilty. In fact, we give the thoughts in our mind more time and attention, which just helps them grow and find similar thoughts, the clustering effect of thoughts attracting similar thoughts we discussed much earlier in the book.

To use a different analogy, if we focus our thoughts on what causes us distress, we give it "oxygen" to attract more of the same. A bit like giving a fire more oxygen, so it burns more fiercely. Instead, just observe the fire, don't judge it, just let it be and it will die down in time because you are not fanning the flames.

Ok, when we are in pain and have a fear, many times we do the equivalent of putting our headphones on, turn up the music and hope it will go away, off course it does not. As we learnt earlier, trying not to think of something does not work. You just end up focussing more on what you are trying to block out, so you cluster more thoughts on the area of your attention.

In Ruby Wax book Frazzled she describes the default process of our brains as an endless loop of having feelings, which turn to thinking about those feelings, which then results in thinking about those feelings. Where the loop starts with feelings or thinking doesn't matter, we can just get caught up in this turmoil thinking and feelings. Ruby's book also supports the idea of placing your attention on your feelings, not the thought, to break this endless loop.

Next time you feel fear or pain over something try this,

So what?

Let your attention rest on the feelings that those negative thoughts create. This is an important and clear distinction, focus on the feelings not the thought itself. Notice where you feel them in your body and just send comforting, accepting feelings in the direction you sense the uncomfortable feeling associated with the thought that is troubling you.

Give unconditional feelings of support.

Notice where in your body you have those feelings. If those feelings move just follow them in your mind's attention. If the feelings change in form, intensity, if they change from being constant to pulsing, whatever they are doing, just observe the feeling and be mentally present with it.

Do not judge the feeling, just accept and acknowledge it. If you are comfortable doing so, send the feeling your love or compassion, unconditionally.

Often people find the intensity of the feeling rises at some point, but just keep going with the process, eventually the feeling subsides and disappears. When you try to recreate the scenario that caused the fear it has either gone or feels much better than before.

By focussing on the feeling and not the thought that created the feeling, you dissolve it, you starve the thought of "oxygen" it cannot grow and increase. You have in fact stopped thinking about the issue or thought, by focussing on its by product, the feeling. In doing this, you achieve the seemingly impossible of not thinking about what is upsetting you, by focussing your attention on the feeling and sending comforting thoughts to it.

Key concept

Once you accept something, it has no power over you and dissipates.

When accepting the feeling, do not include any sense of blame for how you feel. The Roman Epictetus put it as,

"Small-minded people blame others. Average people blame themselves. The wise see all blame as foolishness"

When we have a thought, our minds collect other thoughts to accompany the original ones. We then add our own stories and beliefs to those collection of thoughts. Before long there is a lot of brain stimulation and the original thought has turned into something much bigger and more epic, out of proportion. When our thoughts are positive, we want to enjoy a memory or future dream or solve a problem this can be a great place to be in our minds. When we focus on negative thoughts, it becomes far less comfortable. Because our bodies react the same way to real fear and imagined fear, the impact can be very debilitating. The physically impact can show up in different ways, feeling tense, maybe a headache, uncomfortable feelings in the stomach, feeling stressed and so on. All these physical feelings are simply the mind reacting to your thoughts. Change your thoughts and you change the physical response to these, giving an added feeling of wellbeing.

If you are wondering what these feelings are like, they will be different for everyone and any given thought or situation. The most common feelings are a sensation of tightness or a slightly nauseous feeling. Sometimes the feeling is constant, it can be pulsating, growing or declining in intensity.

Often accepting something can be perceived as just giving in to it, there is a subtle difference, best explained by Michael J. Fox when he said,

> *"Acceptance doesn't mean resignation; it means understanding that something is what it is and that there's got to be a way through it."*

And he added,

"My happiness grows in direct proportion to my acceptance, and in inverse proportion to my expectations."

It's about not fighting the truth of a situation but simply accepting it and deciding how to move forward. For me, this is an important distinction: I do not believe anything is truly impossible. It may, of course, be difficult or take a long time to resolve or change, but it is not impossible in my mind at least. This is my personal belief.

I share this with you simply to illustrate that although I believe that nothing is impossible, I can still accept a hindrance as just being a reality.

I tend to accept something for what it is, without emotion or concern. If that causes me an obstruction in what I am trying to achieve, I believe there must be another way, and I can go around the situation I accept.

To use a simple analogy, I may find a massive, 50-ton boulder blocking my path. Rather than moaning about its existence, I would simply accept the boulder as being in my way and start thinking of ways to best overcome this situation. I could, for instance, go around or over the bolder, retrace my steps and find a different path. My solution is to accept a thing as reality while ensuring that it does not stop me from doing what I want. There may always be another route around this reality.

Eckhart Tolle's interpretation is,

> "Accept – then act. Whatever the present moment contains, accept it as if you had chosen it. Always work with it, not against it."

Some other eloquent interpretations of acceptance are,

> "The only way to make sense out of change is to plunge into it, move with it, and join the dance." –Alan Watts

> "I'm not okay, you're not okay, and that's okay." – William Sloane Coffin

> "For after all, the best thing one can do when it is raining is let it rain." – Henry Wadsworth Longfellow

When we have an uncomfortable or negative sensation in our minds, it translates into how our bodies respond physically as well. Our primal fight or flight system kicks in when we sense fear, be it real or imagined; what matters is how it is perceived. This results in the body's physical response with blood being diverted away from the brain, digestive, and reproductive systems and focused on our ability to fight or run away. Thus, we often feel slightly sick when in fear because of its effect on our digestive system. Because blood is diverted from our brains, our mental capabilities suffer, and the rational part of our brain is somewhat bypassed.

This fight or flight response allows the release of cortisol and adrenaline, which we associate with feelings of stress and can have long-term or short-term effects on our physical wellbeing. Cortisol, meanwhile, suppresses the immune system to reduce inflammation from injuries. This stimulates the amygdala to stay vigilant, which then produces more cortisol; thus, a vicious circle is created. Furthermore, it also suppresses activity in the hippocampus, reducing memory. This means that you can now only think about what you did last time you had a similar emergency.

I have just shared with you a powerful insight and technique regarding how to change your response to negative thoughts. Now let's get back to the main event: Unconditional Love.

The beauty of what I am going to share with you is that the details of what troubles you are not important. You do not have to drag over past issues or analyse them. You also do not have to change your memories or try to understand or interpret those past events. You may find this reassuring since such "investigation" can be uncomfortable or painful. Additionally, because our past is part of us and helps define who we are, it is therefore important and best not tampered with.

I lost my mum to pancreatic cancer when I was 17. We lost her within one week of her diagnosis, three years after she had had breast cancer. I am not unique in having events in the past that have shaped us. Despite how challenging life's events can be, they are part of us. The U2 singer Bono's mum died when he was 14, dying suddenly from a brain aneurysm at her father's funeral. Bono's song about his mum, Iris, has a line that sums up how past events are part of who we are and shape us and how we should accept them and value them for what they are. In fact, Bono believes his mother's death is what drove him to write such heart-felt songs and lyrics. The line in the song I refer to that struck a chord with me is,

"The ache in my heart is so much a part of who I am."

The simple technique I will share with you is a universal comfort regardless of the specifics of any past event that may cause you discomfort. It allows you to still be you and learn from past events if you choose to (that's optional and up to you, not part of the technique). The technique acts as a salve that foregoes the need to know the details of a troubling past memory.

Irrespective of upbringing or mental resilience, we all need love, support, and a good hug does not go amiss. Whatever pain or trauma you may or may not have had in the past, the application of Unconditional Love is a universal comfort. In the case of the person I helped, within a few days of sharing and practicing this technique, they were "transformed", in their own words. A mental burden that had been stopping them from enjoying life had been eased. This burden had been running in the background for most of their life, holding them back in some aspects. From time to time, something would trigger a major, debilitating flare-up.

This technique enabled them:

- To start enjoying life by noticing things. For a long time, their mind had screened their experiences in case they might trigger past traumas – that's the unconscious mind trying its best to protect against similar harm. Using this technique allowed them to live an unfiltered existence once again.
- To find reassurance, they no longer had to be scared of old, debilitating feelings returning.
- To go back and reflect on past events in an entirely safe way and enjoy the good memories that had been blocked off by their mind to protect them.

The effect it had, and still has, is profound. These successes inspired me to share this simple technique.

Many of you might read this and think: "This sounds great, but I don't need it. I'm absolutely fine; nothing dramatic has happened in life that has held me back or side-tracked me."

If this is your reaction as well, I would make a few observations:

- We all have events that have shaped us in life, events we cannot help but reflect on from time to time. They may not be the biggest thing on our minds, but they still affect us imperceptibly.

- If, like me, you were fortunate enough to have experienced Unconditional Love as a child, you might think you have this covered. But would it not be wonderful if you knew a simple way of tapping into and enhancing the gift you already have, at will, to enhance your enjoyment of life and boost your resilience?

This technique focuses on feelings and emotions, the language of the unconscious mind.

6A. THE TECHNIQUE – AN OVERVIEW

T he technique is simple, but do not be fooled into thinking it is not powerful, because it is. Its power comes from the simple fact that it utilises how our minds work in two core ways,

1. By understanding how the unconscious works and how it is different from the rational, conscious parts of our minds – primarily how the unconscious part of the mind reacts in the same way to real and imagined events.

2. By utilising the "language" of the unconscious mind – images and emotion.

We will create a mini-movie in your mind of people and things that represent Unconditional Love for you. We will use the mind's ways of working to enhance this mini-movie, enhancing the outcome by using the same techniques experts use to help people memorise things.

We will then add emotion to this mini-movie, adding some sensory sensations such as touch, sound, and sometimes smell to make this mini-movie truly immersive.

Next, we will use our ability to create habits that embed this mini-movie in our minds, then keep running over it, adding a bit more to it each time. We can then either call on this movie on demand. Better still, we can then keep running it once or twice a day to create a higher level of everyday embedded resilience.

We can then tag this mini-movie with a feeling, image, word, or phrase so we can trigger it at will.

Within a few hours of our conversation with the person I helped, I was able to guide them to "design" their unconditional mini-movie with their own cast of figures representing Unconditional Love. Sometimes it takes a bit of tweaking and practice. Within 24 hours, they noticed big benefits that continued to strengthen the more they practiced the technique.

6B. THE TECHNIQUE – 1ST STEP: CREATE YOUR MINI UNCONDITIONAL LOVE MOVIE

The name of this process might perhaps give the impression that it is complicated; however, it's actually quite easy. Expressing this technique as a process makes it easier to break it down into simple, actionable steps.

The outline of the process, all of which occurs in your mind, is thus:

- **Mini-movie** - create a mini-movie in your mind that demonstrates a story of Unconditional Love – a combination of real and imagined events, or entirely imagined if you prefer.

- **Overlay emotion** – add the sensation of emotion to your mini-movie.

- **Add sensation of touch** – add information about what you feel, as if you are directly in the movie; this step is not essential but can help elevate the effect.

- **Add a soundtrack** – not essential but consider what sounds you hear and what is being said in your mini-movie.

- **Add smell or possibly taste** – it is unusual to be able to add this much detail to your mini-movie, but if accomplished, it can really enhance the experience. Say, for example, that your mini-movie is set outside on the grass on a sunny day; perhaps you can smell fresh grass.

Find somewhere you are safe and will not be disturbed for a while. Get into a relaxed state and think about Unconditional Love. Reflect on experiences you may have had personally, have heard others talk about, or have seen demonstrated in a film. Imagine the sensation of Unconditional Love; let your mind wander, just considering what it is and what it means to you.

Mini-movie

In your mind, you will now start creating a little mini-movie unique to yourself that represents Unconditional Love being bestowed on you. You are the centre of this movie, the lead character. Imagine the movie as if you are participating in it; imagine yourself seeing from what is happening through your own eyes, in first person. Occasionally, however, the film may pan out, allowing you to see yourself in it before returning to first person.

Remember that the movie should mainly be about what you're experiencing directly.

You want to create a movie that truly conveys Unconditional Love. It is your movie: construct the rules of who and what is in your movie, and who does what.

In a moment, I'll ask you a series of questions. You do not have to answer all of them; I only ask them to help you consider what your movie looks like. Let your mind wander. If you find yourself entering a slightly sleepy or dreamy state, all the better: this is the state of mind where you will have the best access to your unconscious mind.

Be creative, abstract, and even absurd if you wish. The movie in your mind does not need to make logical sense; it just needs to make sense to you. For example, your movie can move from one location to another and have people in it who are dead or fictional. The important thing is that everything in your movie should portray your version of Unconditional Love. The theory below gives you an insight into why your movie can be creative.

Theory

The unconscious mind responds well to the same techniques used to enhance memory; these techniques require using images that are:

- *Colourful*

- *Able to convey emotion – the more emotion, the better. Keep it to loving, positive, nurturing emotions*

- *Able to convey movement; remember, movement in this context is better than still pictures*

- *Action orientated, i.e. Include action, doing things*

- *Wacky, imaginative, the more exaggerated or slightly weird they are, the better. Another way of achieving this is to add an extremely specific detail to an image that makes it more distinctive and memorable*

If you can and feel it is appropriate to your mini-movie, humour is a great way of enhancing the impact and recall.

Try to incorporate this into your mental images.

Association – is the easiest and most powerful tool you can use. If you make ensure the elements of your mini-movie already have an association in your mind with what you want to create, you are onto a winner. Association effectively means you have an existing neural pathway, when you link this into your mini movie it is easier to recall, remember and gives a bigger emotional impact. Use the most appropriate associations you already have with the concept of Unconditional Love.

Many people prefer to start creating a movie in their minds immediately; others like to take some notes and then create something from those notes. Do what works best for you.

Here are some questions to reflect on that will help you create your mini-movie.

Who (one or more people) is in your movie?

- Someone real or imagined that has or had a big positive impact on your life
- Someone or something you would have loved to have had in your life that you associate with Unconditional Love
- Parents, grandparents, siblings, aunts, uncles, neighbours, friends, friends' family, a pet, a teacher, someone you admire
- A superhero, a fictional character (film, book, cartoon), or an imaginary friend you may have had when a child
- A famous person you admire
- Someone alive or someone no longer with us
- Someone you think about who you never met (perhaps a grandparent you never knew but think about)
- Someone completely made up in your mind: perhaps someone you wish you had in your life, a combination

of people/characters - perhaps you want different attributes from different people, one person or a group of people?

- Perhaps a sports team, a music band, your sports or local church group, a bunch of friends

What are they doing?

Are they:

- standing up, sitting down, writing, looking up or down at something?
- walking or running towards you?
- doing something with you, like working in the garden
- hugging you?

What do you associate with this scene?

- A place or possession? Specific clothes, glasses, a walking stick or a car- is anything that you can link to them?
- An object that is special to you? It may be a childhood teddy bear, a book someone gave you, a picture, a toy, a favourite tool in your workshop.

One of the most powerful and touching examples I heard of when running a workshop was someone imagining their daughter, an infant at the time, grown up as their source of Unconditional Love for the times when life is challenging. How powerful and wonderful it is for your Unconditional Love to be reflected back on you.

Where is the movie running?

- What place is it? Is it indoors, outdoors, a place you know well?
- Is it a real or imagined place
- Is it a combination of places, i.e. your favourite house and your favourite holiday location?
- Is there a particular occasion? It may be a graduation, a party, marriage, childbirth, or winning a race or competition.
- What is the situation or context? It may be amongst a group of treasured friends, a moment of inspiration, a holiday, or a special moment like a birth or marriage.

Image or images

In keeping with the theme of Unconditional Love, the image or images need to be able to convey Unconditional Love to you. It can be a single image, a combination, or static or moving pictures.

As I mentioned earlier, if you use the same methods that help us memorise, all the better. As such, movement tends to be better for our purpose.

These images should include a person, people, a fictional character, or animals you associate with Unconditional Love. That sense of someone loving you and wanting the best for you, come what may, desiring nothing in return other than seeing you happy. Imagine that person(s) or animal, what they might be saying to you, and how they look and behave.

Are they smiling or waving to you? Interact with them; receiving a hug or a cuddle is a pretty universal winner. Perhaps you might wish to talk to them. It might be specific words or just a sensation of words, with a sentiment. The beauty is that none of this needs to make logical sense; you can make it up. It only needs to mean something to you that is relevant when it comes to conveying your version of Unconditional Love.

Go wild with your imagination. Your images, for instance, could be of an object. For example, you could imagine some golden throne or seat that has infinite energy of Unconditional Love that fills you with some magical Unconditional Love when you sit in it in your imagination. You could imagine this in so many ways; as a warm feeling, some powerful sensation, or feeling the sun's warmth on you. The key is that it can be whatever you want and imagine it to be. The more fanciful or peculiar, the better; this is how the unconscious mind conveys thoughts. If you have ever remembered a dream (I seldom do, but my wife does), you know just how "weird" our dreams can be.

In an attempt to inspire your own mental images, perhaps you can imagine something like a transparent tube or healing dome that you imagine walking into imagining the tube or dome saturating you with Unconditional Love. Or you might have an image of Unconditional Love raining down on you.

Go for it. You can be rational with your ideas if they mean something special and relevant to you; or, you could manufacture something in your mind or combine the real and imagined, rational and irrational.

Overlay emotion

The unconscious mind uses the language of images and emotion. Now let's consider the emotions in this mini-movie. The most important emotion is yours, but you can also consider the emotions of some of the key characters in your movie.

Once again, I stress that your unconscious mind behaves and responds similarly to real or imagined images. Even if your image is based on something real, you can still enhance it and embellish it as much as you want: it is your own personally created image and emotional association. You can play with this to your heart's content. This is not the place for logic, just pure indulgence, and creativity.

What emotions can you sense?

- Love
- Pride
- Hope
- Happiness
- Excitement
- A sense of achievement
- Wellbeing
- Strength
- Invincibility

Consider what other the emotions you want to link with the images you have created, emotions like,

- Absolute and infinite love
- Appreciation
- Acceptance
- Understanding
- Physical comfort
- What does it feel like to be hugged, hold hands etc.?
- Abundance

Now run through the movie in your head; keep repeating and modifying it. Be careful to notice different small details. Now consider and imagine the emotion. As you consider the emotion, imagine turning the intensity up, further, higher, stronger. Perhaps it's waves of emotion, or one constant feeling of emotion, you decide.

Add sensation of touch

What can you feel?

- Can you feel a hug, kiss, or the feeling of someone holding your hand?
- Can you feel the sun's warmth on your face or a cool breeze?
- Do you feel the warmth of a person or animal you are touching in your mind-movie?

Add a soundtrack

Now, let's add some sound to this movie.

- Can you perhaps hear your favourite, or any uplifting song playing in the background?
- Is anyone or anything talking to you? What are they saying?

    They might, for example, say:
    - "I love you"
    - "You're amazing"
    - "That's fantastic"
    - "I'll always love you"

     ○   "I'll always be there for you"

     ○   "I am always with you"

- Do the characters in your story have an accent or do they speak a specific language?

Add smell or possibly taste

This part might not fit well with your movie and isn't essential. But if you can link some smells or tastes with positive memories and feelings attached to them, even better. The smell is one of the most powerful senses for projecting you back into an old memory. I did a workshop on this once, and the company's Managing Director had a small bottle of suntan lotion on their desk, which they occasionally smelled to remind them of family holidays. This is a great way of using smell to propel your mind somewhere special. The other day I finished a jar of Amaretto flavoured coffee that my daughter bought me as a thoughtful Father's Day gift, I have kept the small jar as the smell reminds me of her thoughtfulness.

Some questions that might help your movie creation are as follow.

- Is there food involved? For example, I may imagine the smell of my mum making fresh bread.
- Can you smell the outside, like flowers, grass, the sea, some animals on a farm?

- Does one of your characters have perfume or a distinctive smell of the washing powder they use on their clothes?
- Our pets have unique smells- is that relevant?
- Can you smell or taste an ice cream that reminds you of somewhere special?

In the following chapters, I will share with you how to develop your mini-movie and keep refining and practicing it.

Summary

Create a mini-movie in your mind that conveys Unconditional Love to you. Then add layers to this movie using,

- Emotion
- Sensation of touch
- Techniques used to memorise items.
- Colour, movement, and action
- Absurd elements or exaggeration

6C. THE TECHNIQUE – 2ND STEP: REFINE AND REPEAT

Some people are great at making intensive and colourful mini-movies in their heads, while others struggle with doing so. Either way, it is important to periodically keep running through the movie and refining it. Why?

- It can be fun and beneficial
- As you add more to the mini-movie, it becomes easier to recall and induce on demand
- You make the neural pathway stronger in your mind through repetition and adding more dimensions to it

Think of it as adding more layers. Think about what else you want to add to,

- The characters
- The setting
- The words
- The sounds
- The dialogue
- The emotions and feelings
- Any sense of taste or smell
- The feelings

The best way to do this is spontaneously, or at a regular time, somewhere you are safe and will not be disturbed. Run through the mini-movie in your mind. Be like an editor, reviewing the movies and adding or tweaking parts of them. Just keep refining it and at the same time, enjoying it.

Tip: Rick Hanson's book "Hardwiring Happiness" talks about many aspects of the brain's workings. One way of enhancing memory and aiding recall is to add a level of novelty to images in your mind. To put it another way, add a piece of detail that means something to you. For example, a person in your image is wearing a coat with buttons on. You notice they have five buttons, and five may represent something unique to you, like your birthday, your favourite number, the house number of where you grew up, or how many children you had. You get the idea: a meaningful piece of detail. This adds a hook for you to remember things.

Sub modalities

Another way to enhance your mini-movie is to better define and exaggerate the sub modalities. 'Sub modalities' are the details or embellishments that increase the intensity of your mini movie experience with regards to the five senses. Exaggeration, meanwhile, is how the unconscious mind works; think about dreams and how absurd they can be.

Here are some examples of sub modalities.

Visual	Audio	Touch
Black & White or Colour	Stereo or Mono	Heavy or Light Weight
Sharpness of colour	Fast or Slow	Vibration
Bright or Dim	High or Low Pitch	Smooth or Rough Texture
Clarity (clear/dull/fuzzy)	Verbal or Tonal	Constant or Intermittent
Size of Picture	Rhythmic	Hot or Cold Temperature
Associated (seen through your own eyes) or Dissociated	Timbre (fullness of sound)	Size
Focused or De-focused	Loud or Quiet	Shape
Framed or Unbounded	Pressure	Density
Moving or Still Pictures	Clarity (clear vs muffled)	Natural vs man made
Fast, Normal or Slow Movie	Spoken accents	Human or animal

3-D or Flat	Tonality (flatness)	Duration of touch
Near or Far	Voice language	Constant

Add intensity to the visuals and senses

Now consider increasing the intensity and impact of each sub modality, for example, the intensity of emotion, intensity of colours, the pitch or loudness, or the impact of touch.

Summary

Keep refining your mini-movie, adding more layers, detail, and intensity. Use the five senses' sub modalities to increase your mini movie's impact.

6D. THE TECHNIQUE – 3RD STEP: MAKE IT A HABIT

We have now created our mini-movie in our mind, with the associated emotions and senses. Next, we need to do two things,

1. Keep practicing and rehearsing the mini-movie in our minds
2. Learn how to invoke the mini-movie at will when needed

We can refer to the first approach as "proactive" and the second option as "responsive". Let's clarify the reasoning behind them.

6D.1 WHY PROACTIVE?

If we keep running the mini-movie in our minds, preferably at least once a day, we build mental resilience. Once it grows embedded into us, invoking it at will is much easier and more powerful.

Rehearsing the mini-movie daily gets it ingrained in our minds, and as our unconscious mind takes this literally, it effectively becomes our reality. This, in turn, builds our base resilience and the ability to bounce back quickly from life challenges. Investing this small amount of effort running over our mini-movie daily achieves the following,

- Gives you 5-10 minutes of sanctuary every day that enables you to be calm and have joy in your life

- Builds up layers of resilience, so when you have a bad day, you are more able to deal with it

- Enables you more easily to invoke the mini-movie and at will (responsive) when something happens in life that makes you need an instant shot of Unconditional Love

I will soon show you an easy way of turning this daily rehearsal into an automatic habit. Given time, this turns into an unconscious reinforcement of the mini-movie representing Unconditional Love.

Why Responsive?

Think of this approach as having your very own instant mental first-aid kit. This kit can be deployed at will when something in life upsets you, stresses you, or knocks you off balance. Without anyone else knowing, you now have your very own, on-demand solution. You can then simply invoke your Unconditional Love mini-movie to give you instant relief by changing your normal unhelpful response to whatever has upset, annoyed or worried you.

What do I mean by your normal unhelpful response? When situations occur in life, we respond in a predictable way that is unique and specific to each of us. Over the years, we all develop a learned response to certain situations which is stored as a habit in our unconscious mind. For example, if we see someone or think about someone we dislike, we understandably respond in a predetermined way. In this situation, the response would typically be something like,

- fear
- worry
- concern
- anger

We will probably play out a little scenario in our minds, like a discussion with this person that turns unpleasant and makes us feel uncomfortable. These thoughts generally have emotions attached to them, typically fear, anger, or worry.

Imagine a train running down a track before reaching a junction where someone pulls the lever to divert the train down a different track. That different track is a pleasant place, a place we want to go to and feel safe and happy in. The train represents our thoughts; the track represents the neural pathways that map our habits and responses to situations. If we didn't divert the train, we would have our normal unhelpful or unpleasant response. By proactively practicing our mini-movie, we make it easy to pull the lever to change tracks to the response we want: our mini-movie alongside its associated emotion.

Rather sneakily, we can make use of the same mechanism that automates much of our current habitual response to situations and events, but this time, we will be "programming" the response we want, our representation of Unconditional Love.

As we learned before, a significant proportion of our responses go back to the age of two to six. Some of those responses may well still be useful; others will not. For example, in many cultures, we are taught not to talk to strangers for good reasons. In adult life, this can have different implications; for example, if you work in sales, it may cause some level of stress talking to new prospects. In a social setting, it may impair our ability to mix and make friends when going out and socialising with new people. This is simply a learned behaviour or habit, which you may wish to change. Neuroplasticity shows us we can create new neural pathways; combine this with the theory of habits, and you have the ability to change as you choose to.

Now we will create a new response that we wish to have (i.e. our Unconditional Love mini-movie), using the same automation process our brains use. At first, we will consciously program this new response, but in time, it will become automatic and part of our normal background processes but now using a chosen response.

We all have learnt responses to situations, events, and thoughts. These learned responses are neural pathways created in our brains, which are triggered when we notice something specific: a trigger or a cue. For example, if we see someone we dislike, this cue creates a specific learned response, which might be a feeling of anxiety or negative thoughts that may be unpleasant. This triggered response is very real to us; to simplify it, it isa neural pathway in the brain with an attached emotional response. In a responsive situation, all we are going to do is tap into the existing cue or trigger that is causing us discomfort; however, we will create a new neural pathway response corresponding to the same old cue or trigger. It is a bit like diverting a train on a train track. The new track will soon be well-used and, in time, the old track or path will soon grow forgotten and overgrown through lack of use. I have illustrated this below with two simple models.

Current situation before we change anything, existing neural response set off *(response = train, neural path = train track)*

After we have programmed in a new response as an embedded neural pathway, we get this happening.

When a new neural response is invoked, the original response is ignored and gradually erodes; "grass" grows over the tracks of the unused path.

Another good way to think of this is that we are creating a new association with an existing trigger. Our minds work by linking situations, events to a response we have come to associate with that event or situation, we are simply linking in a new associated response.

The following summarises the process,

1. The start – there is a trigger or cue to the existing response happening. Most of the time, it is just enough to recognise that the response is starting, for instance, a horrible feeling or memory rising up. Or it might be that

you know it is a specific place, person, comment, or something else triggering the response.

2. If we did nothing, the existing neural response would kick in, represented by the horizontal train track.

3. However, we are going to create a new desired response, demonstrated in the diagram above as train with steam (signifying this as our new active response) labelled "new neural response" running along the new neural pathway (the curved train track). This represents our Unconditional Love mini-movie and associated emotions.

4. The final point simply reminds us that given enough time, the new neural response becomes the default, like a frequently used train. In time, the old, now-unused response becomes like an abandoned railway line with grass and weeds gradually growing over it. Eventually, it is forgotten and remains only as a vague memory or shadow from the past that has little or no emotional impact on us. That is why the old response train has no steam coming out of the top, signifying it not being the active response anymore.

This book will simply show you how to consciously create and embed a new response and a new neural pathway.

That's it. Simple, isn't it?

That is why this works: it takes away any need to analyse deep-seated trauma or bad learned experiences. You just need to be aware you have a response you do not want anymore and create a new one. The new response is the mini-movie you have already created. You can use the Unconditional Love mini-movie in any situation when you want to feel better.

6D.2   HOW TO BE PROACTIVE

If you apply the technique in a daily routine, regardless of if you feel any mental discomfort, it will increase your mental resilience and mental wellbeing. You will feel better more often, and your ability to bounce back quicker and be less affected by life's traumas will be enhanced.

Prevention is a proactive approach. With this approach, we can use existing triggers from your everyday life that occur a few times a day as a natural reminder to practice. If you do not develop these or practice often, even the best intentions will be forgotten as life gets in your way. This is of utmost importance so that you can build up resilience and practice the new response regularly.

Everyday reminder triggers fall into two categories,

1. **Random** – things like the phone ringing, a parcel being delivered

2. **Regular** – things that you know will happen each day, how often they will happen, and roughly when. These include things such as brushing your teeth, having breakfast, going to work, opening or closing a particular door

You can, of course, combine the preventative and proactive approaches for the best results. The resilience you build from prevention will reduce the impact of the old response, and when you feel the intensity of the old response starting, you can instantaneously trigger the new response.

6D.3 INTRODUCTION TO HABITS

The habit creation we will now discuss on is much easier than creating a physical habit. What we are concerned with is creating new mental habits, which are much easier to implement. With mental habits, learning tends to be very simple and easy to do. Also, because we will use the brain's natural habit creation process and memory techniques, it is far quicker to apply, embed, and start with habit compared to a new physical skill like learning to touch type, playing guitar, or cycling.

From my experience, a habitual mental routine can take root within a maximum period of days or weeks. As you continue to practice mental habits more and refine them, they continue to grow more powerful. Before long, you can invoke them easily, on-demand, and with little mental effort. I have worked with others who have had powerful transformations in just a few days, although it may take a bit longer depending on how well you "design" your mini-movie. By this, I mean finding a "design" that fits well with your specific way of thinking, your sense of humour, and your sense of Unconditional Love.

6D.4 NEW HABIT/RESPONSE BLUEPRINT

At this stage, I want to give a simple overview of creating a new habitual response; I will then proceed to go into more detail. There are four elements to habit creation.

Before I get into the specifics, be reassured that this is much easier than it may initially seem. Very quickly, you could master this. I will show you the full technique that may give the best results, but to start with, the paired-down approach will be very effective.

In essence, the approach is:

1. **Trigger** – the situation, event, environment, or thought you either want to have a different response to or is your cue to practice your new response, i.e. your mini-movie

2. **Responsive** – if using this to respond to issues as they occur, it is best to identify the current trigger or be aware of when the unwanted response starts.

3. **Proactive** – if your strategy is to develop and build resilience with a preventative approach, choose an everyday trigger to practice your new response. When life gives you its challenges, you'll be more likely to be able to roll with them.

4. **Nudge word, phrase, or image** – sometimes it is enough to notice the trigger situation to invoke your mini-movie. You can also "tag" or associate your mini-movies with a single word, phrase, or the 'first frame' of your mini-movie. Think of this as the key to getting your mini-movie running, similarly to a car key.

I call this a "nudge" because that is what it is, a nudge or gentle push in the right direction.

5. **New response routine** – this is the mini-movie with associated emotions you have created.
6. **Anchor** – learn how to strengthen the embedded new habitual response straight after completing your mini movie.

I will now explain in more detail. I will use the following template now to summarise the process.

1. Trigger
The trigger is the situation, event, person, circumstances, or thoughts that set the habitual mental response in motion. When creating a new habit response, there are two ways of looking at the trigger. 1) **Proactive trigger** – to embed our new habit, we need to practice it. We can use an existing daily everyday event trigger as a cue to practice our habits to avoid putting it off. A trigger may be putting our toothbrush down after brushing our teeth 2) **Responsive trigger** – this is the existing trigger that sets in motion the current unwanted habit or routine that we want to replace

First, we must decide what situation, event, or circumstances we are creating the new habit for. Put simply, when do we want this new habitual response to kick in?

If you are struggling with the concept, some examples might help. Here are some typical situations, events, or thoughts that might trigger an existing undesired response.

- Giving a presentation.
- Going for a long drive or driving somewhere new.
- Meeting a person or team for the first time.
- Having a meeting with someone that makes you feel uncomfortable.
- Going to a location that triggers unpleasant feelings.
- Going to a hospital for a procedure or check.

That specific situation or event will trigger thoughts and associated feelings and emotions. It might be easier to notice the thought type rather than the trigger itself.

Sometimes, it might be simpler to use the presence or awareness of the unwanted thoughts as the trigger for a new response.

2. Nudge word, phrase, or image

Sometimes it is simply enough to be aware of the situation, event, or environment we want to invoke the new habitual response of Unconditional Love. Once you have practiced and embedded the mini-movie response enough, you will find it easy to invoke in your mind.

It can also help to give your new mini-movie a "tag". To put it another way, it is a bit like an identity tag. Something like a specific word or phrase that you associate with your mini-movie. For example, the name of the main "character" in your mini-movie. Or perhaps the name of the setting for your mini-movie.

You can also bring an image to mind that somehow summarises your mini-movie; the most obvious choice is the start "frame" or image of the mini-movie.

Why use a nudge word or phrase? Our conscious minds work well with words. A specific word or phrase is a good way of tagging the new habit to set it off. If the trigger for you wanting to use your Unconditional Love routine is an uncomfortable one, using a nudge word or phrase is a good way of pulling your mind out of the emotion and drama of the start of the unwanted current response, which resides in the unconscious mind.

As words are the preferred language of the conscious mind, it pulls your thoughts briefly out of the realm of the unconscious mind into the realm of the more rational conscious mind, just before going back into unconscious thinking with your new chosen response.

The simple act of awareness with nudge words, will pull your mind out of its unconscious state. In this state, there exists fear devoid of reasoning; a nudge pulls your mind into a conscious state where you can rationalise and get an instant benefit of wellbeing.

3. Mini movie - response

Earlier in the book, we covered how to create your Unconditional Love mini-movie. Once the trigger is noticed, you can let your mini-movie run.

4. Anchor

This is optional. In B J Fogg's book "Tiny Habits", he emphasises what he calls a celebration straight after the habit has been completed. This anchors the habit faster and deeper in his experience. This celebration is something simple: a few self-talk words of congratulation, maybe paired with a physical gesture, an emotion, or a mental image. It must be something that works for you as a mini celebration that you can deploy immediately after you complete your new habitual response.

Now we will go into each element in a bit more detail. If all this sounds a little complicated, be reassured that it isn't. You'll get the hang of it soon.

Here is the summary of the key elements to creating a new response repeated below,

1. **Trigger**
   a. **Responsive**
   b. **Proactive**
2. **Nudge word, phrase, or image**
3. **New response routine**
4. **Anchor**

7. HOW TO CREATE YOUR NEW HABIT – STEP BY STEP

7.1 TRIGGER

For any habit to kick in, it needs a trigger or cue, which is to say a set of circumstances that the mind can detect so that it can perform its functions. It may, for instance, do something like this,

> *When I detect X (the trigger/cue), I will respond unconsciously and do Y (the new habit response – in our case, the mini-movie).*

Here are some simple examples from everyday life,

- When I see my front door (the cue – as I know exactly what my front door looks like), I will reach for my keys (the habitual response).
- When it is dark, AND I enter the bathroom (the cue – in fact two cues combined here), I will reach for the light and turn it on (the habitual response)
- When my mobile phone pings (the cue), I will reach for my phone to see what information I have just received (the habitual response)

The examples I gave are all physical habits. It works just the same way with habitual mental responses, for example.

- When I see person X, I feel happy and smile (this applies to someone you like, admire or love). For other people, you might have a different habitual response i.e.
- When I see person Y, my heart sinks. I start feeling fearful and unhappy
- When I see junction X on the motorway (perhaps on the way to work), I start feeling anxious or maybe happy (depends on if you like work or not)
- I feel sad and lonely when I start thinking about what happened last year on XXX. (The trigger is a specific event that pulls you into the past)

Start noticing some of the triggers to your existing basic routines or habits. Maybe start by considering your daily routines and then look for the triggers. I suggest this not to help the technique specifically but to increase your awareness and understanding of what is happening.

When you start being consciously aware of your daily routines, you will be amazed at how many there are. The whole point of habits is that they run silently, without conscious thought to help automate our lives and get stuff done. These routines are constantly helpful, and that is fine. Because they are automatic, however, we often have routines that do not help us. They might make us feel bad, but they are so deeply embedded we just accept them as part of us.

The trigger is what kicks off a response, either an existing response or a new one.

For now, just start observing your existing habits and what the triggers are to get used to the concept of habit triggers. You do not need to do the next "So what?" task to use this technique, but you might find it useful to increase your awareness.

So what?

Keep a notepad and pen and start noticing your daily routines and the triggers that set them in motion.

Here are some themes to help you find these hidden routines,

- What are your morning routines? – getting dressed, showering, having breakfast, a commute?
- What are your start-of-day routines? – when and how do you switch on your computer? When and how do you make a drink? What task do you do first when you start work?
- What breaktime routines do you have? Where do you have your break and how? What is the trigger for a break?
- What lunchtime routines do you have? Is it always at the same time?
- What coming home routines do you have?
- What evening meal routines occur and why?

- What bedtime habits do you have?

Just start noticing these, and before long, you will be more aware of how our habits are set up and appear. This will help you when you wish to create new habits.

Make a note here,

Trigger	Describe habit routine	Observations?

In the early stages of embedding a habit, we will want to keep practicing it. The more we perform the habit, the better we get at it. As we refine the routine and repetition, we embed the habit into ourselves. It becomes more ingrained and automatic as an unconscious action.

Embedding the habit is creating a new neural pathway in our brains, so we can trigger the response.

There are two types of triggers to consider,

1. Proactive trigger
2. Responsive trigger

7.1.1 Proactive trigger

To practice the habit, we will create a proactive trigger that will remind us without thinking to practice our new habit, which is no more than a mental rehearsal. Choosing an existing event in our lives is much easier than creating a new trigger, such as a reminder in our phone to practice the habit at a certain time. By using an existing trigger, we are tapping into how our extant habits work.

You can choose a trigger that happens regularly every day at a frequency that fits with how often you want to practice your new habit. Always choose a trigger where you are safe to practice your new habit, one that enables you to safely go off into a bit of a dream-like state, similar to daydreaming.

How often should you practice? Once a day is fine, though twice or three times a day is even better. In the early days, the more often you practice per day, the better. When the routine (mini-movie) is nicely embedded, once a day will be enough to build up your overall resilience levels to bounce back from life's many setbacks. Even when you feel the new response is firmly embedded and rehearsed, I strongly suggest you practice it at least once a day, occasionally adding a bit more detail or a new embellishment.

These are examples of the triggers I use and how often they occur a day

- Brushing my teeth – specifically when I put my toothbrush down (twice a day)
- When I sit down in my office seat (multiple times)
- When I touch the fridge handle (twice a day)
- When I type in a password on my computer (multiple times a day)
- When I make a drink (four or five times a day)
- When I put the key in my front door (twice a day)
- When I lock the car (four times a day)
- When I touch my mobile phone (multiple times a day)

In PJ Fogg's book "Tiny Habits", he makes an important point regarding the trigger you use. He believes that the trigger should be very specific and detailed, so much so that there is absolutely no argument or ambiguity as to exactly what when you will enact your new habit. Here are some examples of vague trigger descriptions followed by specific ones.

Vague, open trigger description	Clear trigger description
When I arrive in the office	The first moment I sit in my office seat
When I brush my teeth	When my hand leaves the door handle of the bathroom after I've brushed my teeth
When I get home	The first time I sit down after I get home

7.1.2   Responsive trigger

Once we have practiced a new habit or response, we want to start using it to replace the previous unhelpful response.

Some unwanted habits might be triggered by a range of triggers. These may be a certain environment, such as being in a specific room or with a certain group of people. It may even be a specific time of day.

The easiest trigger is simply the awareness that the old habit is kicking in. You could get specific and work out exactly when you have negative thoughts, perhaps in a particular situation, or when you see a specific person. These are your triggers. Or you may simply use the trigger that currently enables you to have these feelings, thoughts, and responses to invoke your new habit response instantly.

You can then use the nudge to invoke your new response (the mini-movie).

7.2   NUDGES

A nudge is as simple as a tag or index for your new response.

Something you can associate with your new response, as a way of letting your mind know to start the new response when you choose to.

I will show you three variations of how you can do this simply, so you can choose the approach that best suits you. We are all different and so you will find some variations suit you better than others.

The three simple word variations I am going to share with are,

1. Nudge word – a single word
2. Nudge phrase – a few words or a phrase
3. Nudge image

A few examples might help.

Let's say your mini-movie has the key character playing a big role. You can use the name of this character as your nudge word; for instance, you could use the name of your pet as a trigger to evoke a mini-movie containing this pet.

Perhaps your mini-movie is set in a particular place. In this case, you could use a single word or phrase to tag this, for example:

Italy holds 1990

Euro's 2020

Christmas when eight years old

Home with mum

Maybe the nudge word is what's happening in the mini-movie, for instance:

Big hug, laughter, eating, party, celebration

Use an image that sums up your mini-movie. What is the first frame of your movie? It may be an image of a place, person, or location.

7.3 ANCHOR

An anchor is optional. Personally, I find I do not need this, but it reportedly works well with others when it comes to:

- Embedding the new response quicker
- Making the response stronger

Some who write about habit formation talk about putting rewards in place after completing a new habit response. So, for instance, if you create a new habit to start walking for 10 minutes each day, you give yourself some sort of reward at the end of the walk.

In his book "Tiny Habits" B J Fogg refers to this as a celebration. He also argues, however, that rewards do not always work. This is because the rewards sometimes do not follow directly after the habit, so the enhancing benefit is lost. Also, after time, the reward has less effect.

Professor Fogg's approach has the following ingredients,

- Celebration always follows **<u>instantly</u>** after the new habit is completed
- The celebration is simply a combination of
    - **Mental self-praise** – This includes words and phrases such as "well done", "good job", "victory", and "that was special".
    - **Simple physical celebration** – Includes gestures and actions such as a fist pump, a salute, a jump in the air etc.

The concept is simple and effective. The simple act of celebration helps build the new neural path quicker through the principle of rewarding behaviours. Once you feel the new habit is successfully embedded, you only need to perform this celebration/anchor occasionally.

7.4 SUMMARY TEMPLATE

Here is a simple summary template you can use if you want to create your new habit design on a piece of paper. Of course, you could choose to do this as a mental task.

Trigger

The cue that sets off the existing undesired response or the new desired Unconditional Love mini-movie response	
Responsive	**Proactive**
Trigger for an existing event or situation with an undesired current response.	*So that you have a very specific trigger to remind you to practice your new desired response, your mini-movie, remember to be very specific and detailed.*

Nudge

Simple label or tag that you associate with your new mini-movie response to help you invoke it easily, choose either a nudge word or phrase, not both. Adding an image or a feeling enhances the technique but is not essential.

Nudge word	
Nudge phrase	
Nudge image	

New response routine – mini-movie description

You probably will not need to create a written record of your mini-movie as it resides in your mind; if you need to write it down or make some shorthand notes, do it here. When first "designing" your mini-movie, descriptive notes can be useful

Anchor

Record your mental celebration and/or physical response to use straight after you have completed running through your mini-movie routine – P J Fogg's book suggests a verbal celebration followed by a simple physical celebratory gesture.

8. SUMMARY

There we have it, the Unconditional Love technique explained. Here are some thoughts to help tie all of this together.

Do little and often

It is far better to have a little practice and fun with the process and practice once a day rather than try and "perfect" the technique and delay doing anything.

Power of the unconscious

If you still have any suspicions regarding the effectiveness of this process, best to suspend them. The unconscious mind responds the same way to real and imagined thoughts and images, the language of the unconscious mind. You have the opportunity to design your very own Unconditional Love scenario with absolute creativity; in fact, the more vivid and outrageous, the better. The unconscious mind responds well to outlandish imagery, and this would lead to better results in the long run.

9. PROCESS SUMMARISED

How to enhance	Create a mini-movie in your mind
Colourful	
Emotion	- Overlay emotion
Movement	- Add sensation of touch
Action orientated	- Add a soundtrack
Wackey	- Even better if you can....
	- Add smell and possibly taste

Mini-movie creation guide

Who?

- Friends, family, teacher, pet, friends' family, someone you admire
- Superhero, fictional character, imaginary friend
- Alive or dead
- Someone you never met i.e., great grandparents, parents etc
- Sports team, favourite band, church group, social club

What are they doing?

Association

- A possession, an object, a different time

Where?

- Indoors, outdoors, a special place, real or imagined
- An occasion, wedding, birth, birthday, party etc

Somewhere you have been, would   like to go to, somewhere famous
Somewhere special -

Make your new Unconditional Love response a habit, so it becomes

1. Proactive triggers
- Daily practice of mini movie

a) **Random** e.g. when emails come in, when your phones rings (after you hang up on the call)

b) **Regular** – when brushing teeth (when you put your tooth brush down), when locking or unlocking the door to where you live, or your car, or when you get on or off public transport

(Brackets gives examples of being specific for triggers)

1. Responsive triggers

- Enact when current feeling / response to a situation or event makes you feel bad or sad

a) Cause of unwanted current response
b) Sense unwanted response is kicking in

2. Nudge – "label" or "tag" your new response with a Nudge word, phrase or image

3. Run Unconditional Love mini movie in your mind

4. Anchor new response mini-movie

BIBLIOGRAPHY

Austin, A. (1992) *A Safe Self-Help Guide Self Hypnosis*, London: Thorsons

Canfield, J & Hansen M.V. (1999) *Chicken Soup for the Soul*, Chatham: Random House Group

Covey, S.R. (1999) *First Things First*, London: Simon & Schuster

Covey, S.R. (1999) *The 7 Habits of Highly Effective People*, London: Simon & Schuster

Childs, M. (2015) *Speaker Session at Academy for Chief Executives West Midlands Group Meeting*

Amy Cuddy (1st October 2012), *Your Body Language May Shape Who You Are*, Ted Talk. Online. Available
https://www.ted.com/talks/amy_cuddy_your_body_language_sh apes_who_you_are/transcript?language=en

117

Frankl, V.E. (2004) *Mans Search for Meaning*, London: Rider

Ferguson, M (Professor). (13 July 2017), *The Psychology of Success (Speaking at the Academy for Chief Executives)*

HappiMe App, (Published on May 25, 2013), Online with YouTube, Available at
https://www.youtube.com/watch?v=QCnfAzAlhVw

Hartley, S.R. (2012) *How to Shine*, Chichester: Capstone Publishing Ltd

Hartley, S.R. (2015) *Stronger Together*, London: Little Brown Book Goup

Hartley, S.R. (2013) *Two Lengths of the Pool*, Arkendale: Be World Class

Hartley, S.R. (2016-18) *World Class Teams (Speaking at several Academy for Chief Executive CEO sessions)*

Hartley, S.R. (17 May 2018) *World Class Mindset (Speaking at Academy for Chief Executive CEO session)*

King, B. (2010) *How to Double Your Sales*, Harlow: Pearson Education Ltd

McKenna, P. (2015) *Instant Influence & Charisma*, London: Bantam Press

Milgram, S. (1963) *Journal of Abnormal and Social Psychology*, University of Minnesota: American Psychological Association

Murphy, J. (1997) *The Power of the Subconscious Mind*, London: Simon & Schuster UK Ltd

O'Conner, J. & Seymour, J. (2002) *Introducing NLP*, London: Element

Jack Zenger and Joseph Folkman, (15th March 2013) *The Ideal Praise-to-Criticism Ratio*, Harvard Business Review, Online. Available https://hbr.org/2013/03/the-ideal-praise-to-criticism

Tolle, E. (2002) *The Power of Now: A Guide to Spiritual Enlightenment*, Vancouver: Namaste Publishing

Wax, Ruby. (2016) *A mindfulness guide for the Frazzled*, Penguin Random House UK

Wax, Ruby. (2013) *Sane new world*, London, Hodder & Stoughton Ltd

Dean, Jeremy. (2013) *Making habits breaking habits How to Make Changes that Stick*, London, Oneworld Publications

Duhigg, Charles. (2012) *The Power of Habits – why we do what we do how to change*, London, Random House Books

Gawdat, Mo. (2017) *Solve for Happy – engineer your path to joy,* Bluebird

Hanson, Rick. (2013) *Hardwiring Happiness – the practical science of reshaping your brain – and your life,* Rider

Fogg PhD, B J. (2019) *Tiny Habits – The Small Changes That Change Everything,* London, Virgin Books

Brown, Derren. (2016) *Happy – Why more or less everything is absolutely fine,* London, Penguin House

An experiment by Gibson and Walk in the 1960's established that we are born with only two fears.

1.   Fear of falling

2.   Fear of loud noises

http://www.kokdemir.info/courses/psk301/docs/GibsonWalk_VisualCliff(1960).pdf

Gibson, E. J., & Walk, R. D. (1960). The "visual cliff." Scientific American, 202, 67– 71. 2. Fant

ABOUT THE AUTHOR

Matt Sturgess was born on the south coast of England. Despite living a mile from the sea for most of his life, he has not learnt to swim, yet!

He grew up in the biggest Council housing estate in England, an environment where he "learned" a lot about people and survival. He grew up with a wonderful loving family, mum, dad and brother.

Matt started life out as an electronics Honours graduate engineer, then moving on to design the first television surround sound loudspeakers. Matt then enjoyed an international sales career in many big industries, eventually holding roles running businesses.

A deep purpose has always driven Matt to help people. He was often frustrated at school at how many people were written off by teachers telling them they would amount to nothing. Matt's view is simple: each one of us has vast potential. All we need is the right nurturing environment and encouragement, to help realise our potential.

Matt is highly inquisitive and has spent the last decade understanding how the mind works. His aim is to create real, tangible ways for someone to manage their own minds and free themselves to reach their full potential. In essence create a set of "instruction manuals" for how to operate our minds.

Matt now lives in rural Hampshire with his family, having returned to his roots.

RESOURCES

From time to time, I will share some useful resources on my website, mindlocksmith.com

If you need some help and support, contact me through the website.

Above all, I would love to hear your stories of how this book and technique have helped you. Knowing I have helped people is the fuel that feeds my purpose in life, so please share with me your success stories, I would love to hear about every one of them.

Glossary

A few terms I use could have more than one meaning or be ambiguous; the following glossary clarifies these meanings.

Technique

I often refer to the technique. This technique refers to a transformative process broken down into a few steps that enables anyone to have an unconditional story, real or imagined, practiced enough in their mind they can benefit from it anytime.

Mind vs. Brain

On the whole, I use these terms interchangeably, mostly to describe our mental processes. Occasionally, I may use the word brain to talk about the physical attributes or parts of the physical brain. But overall, I use the words mind and brain to talk about our thoughts and how what goes on in our heads works.

Mini-movie

This is my simple label for the mental stories we create in our minds. These stories vary in vividness depending on each person. Some people very much visualize a movie in their minds; for others like me, it is not that exact and is instead a mixture of faint impressions, images, and feelings.

Unconscious mind

The largest and most powerful part of the human mind, the attributes of which I describe in the book. The unconscious is often called the silent or daydreaming part of the mind. It is also sometimes referred to as the subconscious in some books. See the chapter called "Insights into how our minds work" for more on the topic.

Conscious mind

In this book, I describe it as being the reasoning and questioning part of the mind. The conscious mind is the gatekeeper for the more suggestible, unconscious part of the mind.

INDEX

Printed in Great Britain
by Amazon